REBEL WITH A CAUSE

The Daring Adventure of
DICEY LANGSTON
Girl Spy of the American Revolution

by Kathleen V. Kudlinski
illustrated by Rudy Faber

Content Consultant:
Richard Bell
Associate Professor of History
University of Maryland, College Park

CAPSTONE YOUNG READERS
a capstone imprint

icey stretched her tired back. She felt the blue cloth her brother was weaving. "Nice work, Henry. I'll sneak this to the troops when you're done."

Suddenly Colin burst into the room. "I'm a soldier!" He pointed a broom at Henry. "Bang! You're dead!"

Henry spun around, grabbed his chest, and fell over, pretending to be dead. Colin yelled, "Huzzah! I won the war!"

"Stop playing, Henry," Dicey scolded. "Colin, you can do your part for the war by helping us make uniforms. We don't want the soldiers fighting in nothing but boots!"

Little Amy giggled.

Colin pointed to the loom. "But that color is wrong. The soldiers in town wear red coats."

"Can you all keep a sky blue secret?" Dicey put a finger to her lips. "Follow me."

3

Dicey led them to Father's room. "Most people around here like having King George in charge," she said. "But we don't. Our family fights to be free from British rule. We want the liberty to make our own laws. We're Patriots! And Patriots wear blue uniforms."

She opened Father's trunk and pulled out a red, white, and blue flag.

Colin looked out the window. "But the neighbor's flag is different."

"That is Britain's flag," Dicey explained. "Patriots have a new flag. We want to form our own country."

"Pretty stars!" Amy clapped.

"I can count," Bennett said. "Thirteen stars. Thirteen stripes."

"For the thirteen colonies," Henry added proudly.

The door opened. "Laodicea Langston!" Father thundered, using Dicey's full name. "What are you doing? You know the danger!"

"They promised not to tell, Father," Dicey said, quickly closing the trunk.

"What danger, Father?" Colin asked.

Father limped to a chair and sighed. He looked at his children. "We're fighting in secret to free all the colonies on our continent," Father said.

"If our neighbors—the King's Loyalists—found out, they might steal our horses or burn our house." Then he added sternly, "Any of you who spills our secret gets a whipping."

"And you, Dicey," Father said quietly, "no more secret trips to the Continental Army camp. And now you call the horse Liberty? People are beginning to think you are a spy. You know what the Redcoats do to spies."

Dicey shivered. But delivering supplies and carrying messages were her ways to help win this war. How could she just stay home? "I promise to be more careful, Father," she said, looking down at the floor. That was all she could agree to.

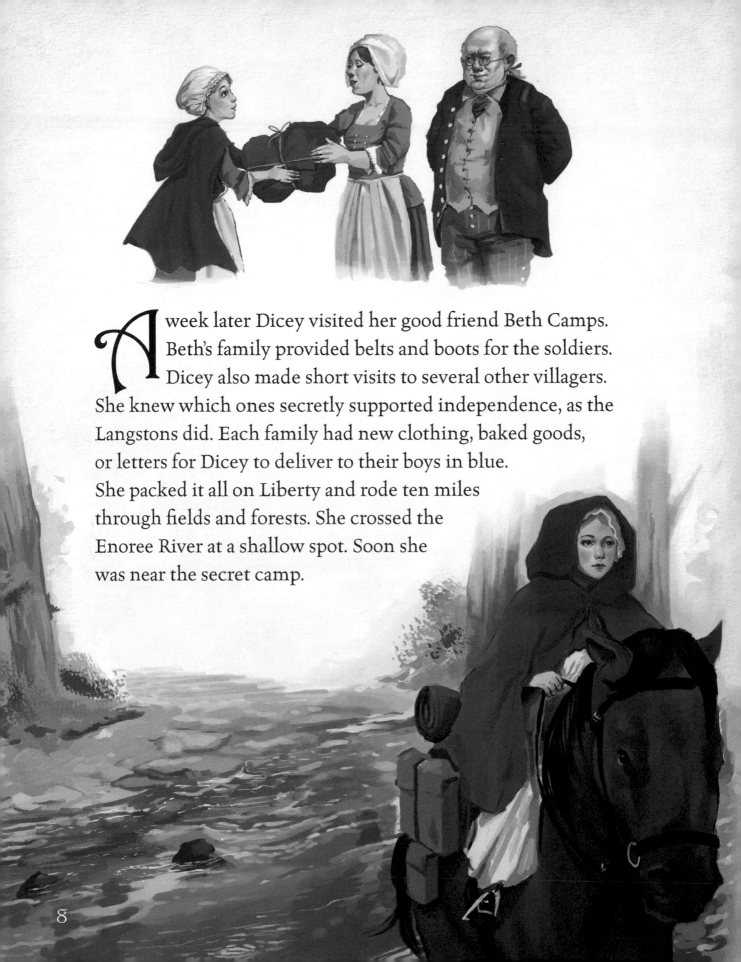

A week later Dicey visited her good friend Beth Camps. Beth's family provided belts and boots for the soldiers. Dicey also made short visits to several other villagers. She knew which ones secretly supported independence, as the Langstons did. Each family had new clothing, baked goods, or letters for Dicey to deliver to their boys in blue. She packed it all on Liberty and rode ten miles through fields and forests. She crossed the Enoree River at a shallow spot. Soon she was near the secret camp.

"Halt, little girl!" a soldier said.
"I'm no little girl, sir," Dicey
answered. "I'm a messenger. You
know my brothers, James and
Solomon Langston."

"So you are Daring Dicey," he
said with a smile. "Your brothers
are fine soldiers."

He rode next to her. "You should
not be out alone. The Redcoats could
see you, or even worse, Bloody Bill
could attack you. I'll escort you
into camp."

9

Dicey handed packages of supplies to grateful soldiers. Solomon hugged her. "Any news from home?"

"We are all well, though Father's old wounds hurt," Dicey said. "Beth sends her love," she added with a smile.

Solomon blushed. "We will marry in June, but that's a secret."

Dicey clapped her hands in joy. "I hoped as much! Are you planning a party?"

"I'm too busy training eight new soldiers!"

James walked up to them. "Hush. The less she knows, the better." He tugged a curl loose from Dicey's cap. "Does Father know you're here?"

Dicey quickly tucked her hair back under cover. "Come home and ask Father yourself. The little ones miss you."

"Too dangerous. You know that," Solomon said. "The Redcoats know we are rebel soldiers, but they think we cut all our family ties. We visit home, and they will suspect Father is a Patriot too."

"By coming here, you risk even more," James added. "Please be careful and leave by another path."

Dicey nodded solemnly. "I'll take care, brothers. But I am in this fight until we win independence."

Dicey had almost made it safely home when she heard horses coming up behind her. She turned to look and gasped. Redcoats! She kicked Liberty into a gallop, but the soldiers overtook her. The tall one grabbed her horse's rein.

"Whoa!" he said, pulling her to a stop. "Have you been to the rebel camp, Missy?"

"Never." Dicey struggled to keep her voice from shaking.

The other soldier pointed his pistol at Dicey's head. "I don't believe you. Where are they? Who is there? What are they planning?"

"I don't know, sir." Dicey could barely breathe. What had that patriot guard called her outside his camp? A 'little girl'? "I'm just a little girl. I like riding sweet Li ..." She stopped mid-word. Her horse's name would give her away! Dicey patted Liberty's mane a moment before finishing. "I love riding my sweet little ol' Daisybelle."

The soldier kept his gun trained on Dicey.

"Go easy, partner," the tall one said quietly. Then suddenly he swept his arm up under the gun. It fired over Dicey's head. Her horse jumped and Dicey galloped away while the soldiers argued. Her heart didn't stop pounding until she reached home.

Two rainy weeks later, Dicey stood dripping at Beth Camps' door with a package.
"A gift?" Beth asked.
"A wedding gift!" Dicey exclaimed.
Beth's face brightened with joy.
"Solomon told you, didn't he?"

"You saw young Solomon? He's alive?" Mrs. Camps cried. "Thank goodness! I worry so about that boy. There is death and danger everywhere these days. And now we hear Bloody Bill is coming to South Carolina."

"Bloody Bill?" Dicey asked with alarm. "When did you hear this?"

"In the crowd after church yesterday. Someone said Bill's band was killing Patriots along a path in North Carolina. They are camped by the border."

"That is just two days' march away ..." Dicey sprang to her feet. "I must be going!"

Back home Dicey thought about Bloody Bill as she prepared supper. People said he had been a good soldier at first. But he began to love violence even more than he loved the Loyalist cause. Now he used his Redcoat uniform to get away with terrible cruelty and murder. The men who rode with him were just as heartless.

Dicey shuddered. Bloody Bill would attack her brothers' camp tomorrow! Who could warn them? Father wanted her safe at home. But he could not ride in this weather himself. And Henry was too young.

"I will have to go," she said out loud. "Tonight."

"Where?" Colin asked.

Dicey looked up with a start. "To bed, of course!"

After supper Dicey pretended to go to bed. She waited under the covers, thinking. *I can't take a lantern tonight. Bloody Bill might see the light. And horse hooves make too much noise. I'll have to walk. I'll wear Mother's old waterproof cape.*

At last the only sound was the rain pattering on the roof. She slipped out of bed. There was a long journey ahead.

Dicey stepped into the dark,
stormy night. *Hurry!* she told herself.
She ran through the wet fields and
woods until her legs ached. Dicey
stopped to lean against a tree trunk.
Her eyes closed. *NO!* She woke
herself, took a deep breath, and
ran on.

At last she heard the gurgling,
rushing Enoree River ahead. She
stepped into it. But when water filled
her boot, she stopped to think.

If my skirt and petticoat get wet, they'll drag me down into the water. I could drown. She shuddered, wishing she could swim. *But I must warn them!*

Dicey looked both ways in the dark, then took off her long skirt and petticoat. Standing in her thin white shift and boots, she wrapped the clothes in her cape and waded into the cold, wild river. Soon she was waist-deep. The dark current fought to sweep her away. *Keep going,* she told herself.

Surging water rose to her neck. "One more step," she whispered. "One more."

A rock shifted. Her foot slipped. There was suddenly nothing under Dicey but water.

"No!" Dicey screamed and choked on the rushing water. The current tumbled her downstream.

Finally she felt stones under her feet again. Dicey stood up in the water, gasping for air. Her teeth chattered with cold and fear. It was dark all around. *Where is the shore? Which way is the camp?*

Dicey wanted to cry, but what good would that do? No. *I have to save them!* She made herself calm down. With surprise she realized she was still clutching her bundle of clothes!

She felt the current pushing her on one side. That told her which way to go. The rain was easing as she struggled up the riverbank. She caught her breath, pulled her wet clothes back on, and hurried into the forest.

At last Dicey staggered into camp. "Solomon!" she called. "James! It's Dicey. Everyone get up!"

Around her, men yelled from inside their tents. "We haven't slept in two days!" one mumbled.

A familiar voice called, "Dicey? What's wrong? What are you doing here?"

"Solomon!" Dicey cried. "Bloody Bill is coming!"

Solomon stumbled out of his tent. He yawned and rubbed his eyes. "What are you doing here in the middle of the night?" he asked. "Bill is many days' ride away. We'll get up at dawn."

"No. Bill will be here today!" Dicey insisted, taking charge. "Get up. Hurry! Rip some wooden shingles off that shed. Find me some dry wood. I'll build up the fire and make you breakfast."

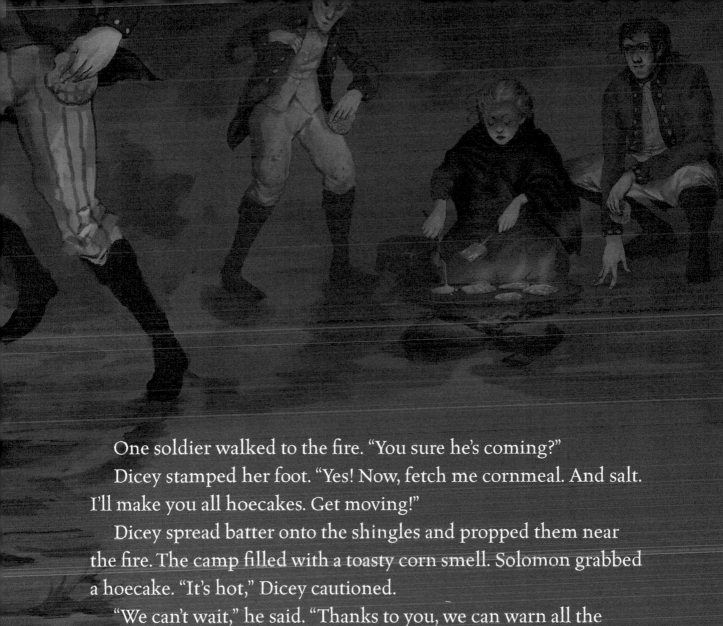

One soldier walked to the fire. "You sure he's coming?"

Dicey stamped her foot. "Yes! Now, fetch me cornmeal. And salt. I'll make you all hoecakes. Get moving!"

Dicey spread batter onto the shingles and propped them near the fire. The camp filled with a toasty corn smell. Solomon grabbed a hoecake. "It's hot," Dicey cautioned.

"We can't wait," he said. "Thanks to you, we can warn all the Patriot families in Little Eden." Soldiers grabbed handfuls of cakes and hurried off into the forest.

James gave Dicey a bear hug. "You've saved our lives tonight, Dicey, and probably many others. Be careful going home, little hero." Then he was off.

Exhausted, Dicey ate the last crumbs. She spread out the fire, sprinkled water on the embers, and began the long walk home. *Little hero*, she thought and shook her head. *I was just doing my part.* But still, the words made her feel warm and happy.

Though she was tired, the return trip was easier. The rain stopped and the sky began to brighten. Dicey could see where to cross the river at the shallow part. Then she ran across the fields and snuck into the house through the kitchen door, cold but nearly dry.

No one was up yet. Dicey sighed in relief. If Father knew she'd gone, he would be angry that she had put herself in danger again.

Dicey yawned and made a cup of tea. Then she made a proper cornbread batter. By the time Father limped downstairs, breakfast was ready.

"You look tired," Father said.

"I couldn't sleep," Dicey answered,
not meeting his eye.

"Hot cornbread!" Henry sat down
and dug in. "I wish Solomon and
James could have some!"

Dicey almost laughed.

The next day Dicey walked to the village to visit Beth. A noisy crowd had gathered on the green. Dicey sat down nearby, patting her dog and listening.

"Did you hear?" Dicey heard one woman ask. "Bloody Bill attacked Little Eden yesterday, but nobody was home. No people. No horses or cows. Nothing valuable."

"Some dirty rebel must have warned them," the woman's friend said with disgust. "Did Bill find the camp and kill the rebel scum?"

"He burned cabins and barns and tents and even poisoned their wells. But he couldn't find anyone to kill. Heard he went purple with rage," the first woman reported.

"Hush!" her friend hissed. "It's that Langston girl."

Dicey buried her face in the dog's fur to hide her smile.

Weeks later a handful of rough-looking Loyalist soldiers pushed their way into the Langston house.

"Old Solomon," the leader said, aiming his pistol at Father's heart, "someone saw your son James in a rebel raid on our supplies. We know you are a spy."

"Stop!" Dicey stepped in front of the gun. "Don't hurt him!"

"Move, girl," another soldier ordered, "or he'll send a shot straight through your heart and your father's too."

Dicey whipped off her scarf so the Redcoat could take better aim. "Go ahead," she dared him. "Shoot." Dicey held her breath and stared into his eyes.

No one moved.

"Well, boys," the soldier finally broke the silence. "I've met my match. This little lady is as crazy as I am." He lowered his gun. "I think I'll let you live, Miss. You and Old Solomon too."

He spit, then turned and left, his men following in stunned silence.

Dicey spent the next month making new clothing to replace what Bloody Bill had burned as he gutted the Continentals' camp. She gathered more supplies from her neighbors too, and hid them under her bed. One day as she was sorting them, she was surprised by Father's voice behind her.

"I'm guessing those aren't wedding gifts ..." he said. Dicey startled and bumped her head on the bed frame.

"No," she admitted, then pressed her lips together.

Old Solomon looked at his daughter. After a moment he said, "I am very proud of what you've been doing. Just please don't tell me about it. My old heart can't take the worry." Dicey gave her father a big hug.

The next day Dicey rode up the ridge above the Tyger River, toward the new camp. James stepped out through the trees to meet her. "I'm on guard duty today," he explained. "May I escort you to camp, birthday girl?"

Dicey smiled, surprised that he remembered. "Now that I'm fifteen, I can do even more against the King," she said.

"Aren't you doing enough, little hero?" he asked.

"Never!" Dicey said.

"Then I have a favor to ask," James said. "Hide this rifle at home. A Patriot leader will come for it soon. His password will be 'Daring Dicey.'"

"Oh, James!" Dicey blushed.

arly one morning, as promised, a handsome young captain came to the door with a group of his men.

"Are you Dicey?" he asked with a smile. "James said you have something for me."

"I have it right here." Dicey got the rifle from its hiding spot. But when the captain reached for it, Dicey paused. "Say the password first."

"A password? Who needs it?" the captain teased. "You've shown us the gun. What's to stop us from taking it?" His men laughed and elbowed one another.

Dicey aimed the rifle squarely at the captain's head. Suddenly no one was laughing.

"Oh, Daring Dicey," he whispered. "You are as brave as any soldier!"

The young captain left with the gun. Next time he would know better than to tease Dicey Langston.

On June first everyone gathered at Beth's house for the wedding. "I want to make a toast." James raised his cup of cider to the new couple.

"Hear! Hear!" the families shouted.

Dicey stood up and raised her cup to the flag. "Another toast. The Patriots are winning battles—we are going to win this war. Three cheers for independence!"

"Huzzah! Huzzah! Huzzah!"

"I want a star," Amy pointed to the flag.

"Put time and work and love into our country, and you'll earn one of those stars." Dicey gave her sister a squeeze.

"Huzzah!"

Dicey Langston was born on May 14, 1766. Revolutionary War battles started when she was nine years old. At that age she would never have guessed that a monument would someday be raised in her honor in her hometown. She'd have been surprised that The Daughters of the American Revolution would make a medal with her likeness. And Dicey, who never went to school or learned to read, would be astonished that 240 years later, a middle school would be named for her in Greenville, South Carolina.

Six months after the events in this book took place, the last battle of the war was fought at Yorktown, Virginia. The soldiers began to go home. Bloody Bill fled to a tropical island to escape punishment for his crimes and murders. Some historians believe he was the man who came to the Langston house, threatening to kill Dicey and her father. History can verify that when the enemy soldiers arrived at Dicey's door, she faced them with courage.

Two years later, on January 9, 1783, Dicey Langston married Thomas Springfield, a Patriot soldier. Many people think Thomas may have been the young captain who came to the Langston home for James' rifle.

The final peace treaty between Great Britain and the new United States of America was signed on September 3, 1783, giving the United States independence. For his service Thomas was given 100 acres of land south of Travelers Rest, South Carolina. He and Dicey built a cabin there and lived a long and happy life, raising 22 patriotic children. As an old woman, Dicey often boasted that she had 32 sons and grandsons who would vote or fight for liberty. On May 23, 1837, Dicey Langston died at age 71, an American Patriot to the end.

CONTINENTAL CORNBREAD

The "hoecakes" Dicey made for the Continental soldiers likely would have consisted only of cornmeal, water, and salt. Colonial cooks added other tasty ingredients to that basic recipe, giving it a little sweetness. This cornbread recipe may be closer to what Dicey would have made in her kitchen.

Ingredients:

1 cup (240 mL) flour
2 tablespoons (30 mL) sugar
4 teaspoons (20 mL) baking powder
1 teaspoon (5 mL) salt
1 cup (240 mL) yellow cornmeal
2 eggs
1½ (360 mL) cups milk
4 tablespoons (60 mL) butter, melted

Instructions:

1. Preheat the oven to 450°F (230°C).
2. Grease a 9 x 5-inch (23 x 13-cm) loaf pan.
3. Sift flour, sugar, baking powder, and salt together. Mix with cornmeal.
4. Whisk the eggs in a small bowl.
5. Add the eggs and milk to the dry ingredients. Stir until moistened.
6. Stir in the melted butter.
7. Pour the mix into the greased pan and bake for 25 minutes. When it's ready, the top of the bread will be golden brown.
8. Remove cornbread from the oven and let it cool for 5 minutes.
9. Serve with honey or butter.

READ MORE

Harness, Cheryl. *Flags Over America: A Star-Spangled Story.* Chicago: Albert Whitman & Company, 2014.

Otfinoski, Steven. *Patriots and Redcoats: Stories of American Revolutionary War Leaders.* North Mankato, Minn.: Capstone Press, 2015.

For more information on key terms of the Revolutionary War, please visit www.capstonepub.com/DiceyLangston

About the Author

Kathleen V. Kudlinski is the author of 40 children's books, ranging from picture books to young adult novels. When not writing, she is a popular speaker and writing instructor. Building on a degree in biology and six years of classroom teaching experience, Kathleen later trained as a "Master Teaching Artist" with the Connecticut Commission on the Arts. Now she eagerly Skypes with classroom, book, and homeschool groups worldwide. Kathleen lives beside a deep, wild lake in Connecticut—and sometimes at a woodland cabin in Vermont—with her naturalist husband, a sweet old pit bull, and a rescue macaw.

Capstone Young Readers are published by Capstone, 1710 Roe Crest Drive, North Mankato, Minnesota 56003
www.capstoneyoungreaders.com
Editor: Kristen Mohn
Designer: Aruna Rangarajan
Creative Director: Nathan Gassman
Production Specialist: Tori Abraham
The illustrations in this book were created digitally.

Library of Congress Cataloging-in-Publication Data
Kudlinski, Kathleen V.
Rebel with a cause: the daring adventure of Dicey Langston, girl spy of the American Revolution/by Kathleen V. Kudlinski; illustrated by Rudy Faber.
pages cm. — (Encounter)
Summary: "Tells the story of a young Revolutionary War hero, Dicey Langston, who warned the Patriots of an attack by the brutal Loyalist leader 'Bloody Bill' Cunningham"— Provided by publisher.
Audience: Grades 4–6.
ISBN 978-1-4914-6073-3 (library binding) — ISBN 978-1-62370-427-8 (hardcover) — ISBN 978-1-4914-6558-5 (paperback) — ISBN 978-1-4914-6559-2 (ebook pdf)
1. Langston, Laodicea, 1766–1837—Juvenile literature. 2. Women spies—United States—Biography—Juvenile literature. 3. Spies—United States—Biography—Juvenile literature. 4. United States—History—Revolution, 1775–1783—Secret service—Juvenile literature. 5. United States—History—Revolution, 1775–1783—Biography—Juvenile literature. 6. United States—History—Revolution, 1775–1783—Participation, Female—Juvenile literature. I. Faber, Rudy, illustrator. II. Title. III. Title: Daring adventure of Dicey Langston, girl spy of the American Revolution.
E280.L36K84 2015
973.3'85092—dc23 [B]   2015004552

Design Elements: Shutterstock: BellonaAhillia, emo_O, Fedorov Oleksiy, Megin, Pola36

Printed in the United States   5648